THIS LAND CALLED AMERICA: **OREGON**

CREATIVE EDUCATION

Published by Creative Education
P.O. Box 227, Mankato, Minnesota 56002
Creative Education is an imprint of The Creative Company
www.thecreativecompany.us

Design by Blue Design (www.bluedes.com)
Art direction by Rita Marshall
Book production by The Design Lab
Printed in the United States of America

Photographs by Alamy (AGStockUSA Inc., All Canada Photos, David R. Frazier
Photolibrary, Inc., Dennis Frates, North Wind Picture Archives, PCL, Greg
Vaughn), Corbis (James L. Amos, Roland Gerth/zefa, Lake Country Museum,
Robert Landau, Warren Morgan, David Muench, Robert Y. Ono, Michael T.
Sedam, Craig Tuttle), Getty Images (Cameron Browne/NBAE, J.R. Eyerman//
Time & Life Pictures, MPI, Time & Life Pictures, Gary Vestal)

Copyright © 2010 Creative Education
International copyright reserved in all countries. No part of this book may be
reproduced in any form without written permission from the publisher.

Library of Congress Cataloging-in-Publication Data
Bodden, Valerie.
Oregon / by Valerie Bodden.
p. cm. — (This land called America)
Includes bibliographical references and index.
ISBN 978-1-58341-790-4
1. Oregon—Juvenile literature. I. Title. II. Series.
F876.3.B63 2009
979.5—dc22   2008009521

First Edition
9 8 7 6 5 4 3 2 1

This Land Called America

OREGON

Valerie Bodden

Oregon

VALERIE BODDEN

A BLANKET OF FOG COVERS THE LOW, ROUNDED MOUNTAINS OF THE OREGON COAST RANGE. THE SHARP SCENT OF PINE FILLS THE AIR. SUDDENLY, A LOUD RUMBLE BREAKS THE STILLNESS. HUGE MACHINES MOVE UP AND DOWN A STEEP MOUNTAIN SLOPE. THEY CUT DOWN ONE TREE AFTER ANOTHER. SOON, THE HILLSIDE IS BARE. BUT IT WON'T REMAIN THAT WAY FOR LONG. NEW TREES WILL SOON BE PLANTED. THE COOL, WET WEATHER OF THE PACIFIC NORTHWEST WILL HELP THE TREES GROW. EVENTUALLY, A NEW FOREST WILL TOWER OVER THE HILLSIDE. ONE DAY, IT TOO WILL BE HARVESTED. ITS WOOD WILL BE USED TO MAKE PAPER, FURNITURE, AND HOMES FOR PEOPLE AROUND THE WORLD.

YEAR
1778 British explorer Captain James Cook lands on Oregon's coast and trades with the Chinook Indians.
EVENT

The Trail West

Long before white people arrived in Oregon, the land was inhabited by American Indians. Most of the Indians, including the Chinook, lived along the coast of the Pacific Ocean. The ocean offered salmon and trout to eat, and dense forests provided deer to hunt and berries to gather. Farther east, the Modoc and Nez Perce settled

Daring explorer James Cook (above) encountered many American Indians in fishing camps along Oregon's shores (opposite).

along streams. They hunted buffalo and deer and also ate plant roots and berries.

Beginning in the mid-1500s, Spanish and British ships sailed along the Oregon coast. But it wasn't until 1778 that famed British explorer Captain James Cook landed on the coast of Oregon. There, he traded with the Chinook Indians. They gave him seal and sea otter fur in exchange for knives and brass buttons. Cook then sailed on to Asia, where he discovered that the furs would sell for high prices.

YEAR

| 1792 | American trader Robert Gray sails from the Pacific Ocean into the Columbia River. |

EVENT

In the early 1900s, descendants of the Oregon Trail pioneers celebrated their ancestors' achievements.

State bird: western meadowlark

Oregon Trail celebration

In 1792, American Robert Gray sailed up a river off Oregon's coast. He named the river Columbia, after his ship. Then, in 1805, an American exploration party led by Meriwether Lewis and William Clark reached the Pacific coast of Oregon by land. They had traveled more than 2,000 miles (3,220 km) from Missouri. When Lewis and Clark returned east the next fall, they spread word of Oregon's fertile lands and furbearing animals.

Britain and the United States laid claim to the region both countries called the Oregon Country. Soon, people from both nations set out for the territory, which covered the entire Northwest. Many of the settlers were "mountain men" who trapped beavers and other animals for their fur. This part of Oregon's history has been honored in the state's nickname as "The Beaver State."

Although the fur trade declined in the 1830s, people continued to come to Oregon. Beginning in 1842, thousands of Americans set out on the Oregon Trail. Walking beside covered wagons filled with supplies, they crossed prairies, mountains, deserts, and rivers. They finally arrived in Oregon City, Oregon, after what was usually a six-month journey.

By 1846, the growing number of American settlers in Oregon led the British to give up their claim on the Oregon

YEAR

1805

EVENT

Explorers Meriwether Lewis and William Clark reach Oregon by land.

- 9 -

Chief Joseph spoke out against the U.S.'s unfair treatment of Indians until his death in 1904.

Country south of what is now the U.S.-Canada border. In 1848, the U.S. created the Oregon Territory. It included the present-day states of Oregon, Washington, and Idaho, and parts of Montana and Wyoming.

The discovery of gold in California and Oregon in the 1840s and 1850s brought more people west. Others came to farm the area's rich soil. By 1859, Oregon had a population of more than 52,000. On February 14 of that year, Oregon became the 33rd state in America. Its capital was Salem.

With more people arriving in Oregon every year, conflicts with the American Indians became more common. Many Indian groups were forced onto lands called reservations that were set aside for them. In 1877, the Nez Perce, led by Chief Joseph, rebelled and headed toward Canada. The U.S. Army followed, and the Nez Perce eventually surrendered. They were moved to a reservation in present-day Oklahoma.

In the 1880s, the railroad came to Oregon. This allowed wood from Oregon's new logging industry to be shipped east. It also enabled people to travel to the state more easily. By 1900, Oregon's population had reached more than 413,000 and was quickly growing.

At railroad stations, logs were stacked on top of flatbed cars and pulled by special logging trains.

YEAR
1811   John Jacob Astor founds Astoria, the first permanent American settlement in Oregon.
EVENT

- 10 -

Pacific Wonderland

OREGON IS LOCATED IN THE PACIFIC NORTHWEST region of the U.S. THE WAVES OF THE PACIFIC OCEAN SPLASH ONTO THE STATE'S WESTERN COAST. WASHINGTON BORDERS THE STATE ON THE NORTH, AND IDAHO SITS TO THE EAST. TO THE SOUTH LIE CALIFORNIA AND NEVADA. OREGON'S VARIED LANDSCAPE CAN BE DIVIDED INTO FIVE MAIN REGIONS: THE COASTAL REGION, THE WILLAMETTE

Valley, the Cascade Mountains, the Columbia Plateau, and the Great Basin.

Mount Hood last erupted in 1865, and some scientists think it could erupt again by 2040.

Oregon has more than 360 miles (580 km) of coastline. In some areas, long beaches stretch along the shore, while in other places, sheer cliffs tower above the water. Bordering the coast are the tree-covered mountains of the Oregon Coast Range. Farther south are the rugged Klamath Mountains. Both mountain systems are part of the larger Pacific Coast Range, which runs from Alaska to Mexico.

To the east of the Coastal Region lies the Willamette Valley. The Willamette River winds through this 115-mile-long (185 km) and 30-mile-wide (48 km) stretch of fertile land. About 70 percent of Oregon's population lives in this region.

The Cascade Mountains tower over the eastern side of the Willamette Valley. The western slopes of the Cascades are covered with thick forests of fir and spruce. Thinner forests of ponderosa pine grow on the mountains' eastern slopes. Within the Cascades stand many inactive volcanoes, including Oregon's highest peak, the 11,239-foot (3,426 m) Mount Hood. Crater Lake, the deepest lake in the U.S., is also found in the Cascades. In 2000, its maximum depth was found to be 1,949 feet (594 m).

Oregon's coasts are known for their sea stacks, the tall columns of rock found near the shore.

YEAR

1842   The first large group of pioneers sets out from Missouri on the Oregon Trail.

EVENT

N ortheastern Oregon is dominated by the Columbia Plateau. Although this region is mainly flat, it does contain the jagged Blue Mountains. Hells Canyon, along the Idaho-Oregon border, is also located there. Reaching depths of more than a mile (1.6 km), it is the deepest canyon in America. South of the Plateau, the flat, dry Great Basin consists mostly of desert.

　　With so many different environments, Oregon is home to a wide variety of animals. Sea otters and sea lions live along the coast. Elk, deer, and mountain lions roam the mountains of the west. Pronghorn, mule deer, and coyotes live in the east.

With their thick fur coats, sea otters (above) can survive in the ocean year-round, while land-dwelling animals such as bighorn sheep and black bears live well in the Hells Canyon area (opposite).

YEAR

1848   The U.S. government establishes the Oregon Territory in the Pacific Northwest.

The Columbia River flows south from Canada and forms part of Oregon's northern border with Washington.

About half of Oregon's land is covered in forests, and trees are the state's most important natural resource. Many of Oregon's forests are logged, making Oregon the number-one producer of lumber in the U.S. Oregon's powerful rivers, such as the Columbia, are also important to the state. Dams on these rivers use the energy from falling water to make electricity. In addition, sand, gravel, and gold are important resources mined in Oregon.

The richness of Oregon's soil makes it ideal for growing trees and crops. The state produces more Christmas trees, hazelnuts, raspberries, blackberries, peppermint, and grass seed than any other U.S. state. Most of Oregon's farmland is located in the Willamette Valley, but fields of wheat and hay can also be found on the Columbia Plateau.

Oregon has two distinct climate regions. West of the Cascades, the climate is mild and wet. It rains about 150 days a year in some locations. To the east of the Cascades, the climate is dry, and temperatures are more extreme, sometimes dropping below 0 °F (-18 °C) in the winter and rising above 90 °F (32 °C) in the summer.

Fresh blackberries are both tasty and healthy, as they are rich in vitamin C and are a good source of fiber.

YEAR
1859   On February 14, Oregon becomes America's 33rd state.
EVENT

- 17 -

Growing Opportunities

THE FIRST SETTLERS TO ARRIVE IN OREGON CAME IN SEARCH OF FUR. AFTER THE FUR TRADE DECLINED IN THE 1830S, FARMING BECAME MORE IMPORTANT. BY 1900, FISHING AND LOGGING WERE ALSO MAJOR INDUSTRIES. MODERN OREGONIANS WORK IN FARMING, FISHING, LOGGING, AND MANY OTHER INDUSTRIES.

Commercial fishing boats use nets, lures, or traps to catch certain kinds of fish and sea creatures.

Today, more than 85,000 people in Oregon work in the logging industry. Some cut down trees, using big machines called harvesters or feller bunchers. Others help make wood products such as paper and furniture. The logging industry has declined in recent decades, partly because of laws that prevent logging in areas where endangered animals such as the spotted owl live.

The fishing industry has also declined due to laws that protect certain kinds of fish, including salmon. But commercial fishing boats can still be found off Oregon's shores. They bring in 150,000 tons (136,000 t) of salmon, snapper, sole, whiting, shrimp, and other seafood each year.

Early loggers had to put logs into position to float down a river, but now trucks transport the logs.

In addition to fishing boats, cargo ships can also be found in Oregon's waters. Huge ships sail from the Pacific Ocean and up the Columbia River to Portland. Some carry electronic products, clothing, and tires into the city. Others carry grain, machinery, and paper from Oregon to other parts of the world.

YEAR

1877 The Nez Perce Indians surrender to the U.S. Army and are forced onto a reservation.

EVENT

Oregon's scenic landscapes and beautiful waterways have also made the state a growing center of tourism. Today, the tourism industry brings $8.3 billion to the state each year. More than 90,000 Oregonians are employed in restaurants, hotels, and other businesses that cater to tourists.

Other jobs in Oregon are tied not to the state's natural resources but to manufacturing. Factories in Oregon make everything from plastics and food products to electronics and scientific equipment. Employees at high-tech companies such as Hewlett-Packard and Intel make computer and printer parts.

With so many different types of jobs, Oregon continues to attract newcomers. Many of them choose to settle in Portland. Because of its mild climate and beautiful surroundings, Portland is often rated as one of the best U.S. cities in which to live. Today, more than a third of Oregon's population of 3.7 million lives in Portland and its suburbs.

The majority of the people in Oregon are white. Some of them are descended from families who traveled to the

In downtown Portland, all that can be seen are tall buildings and lighted signs (opposite), but a wider view shows Mount Hood in the distance (above).

YEAR

1902 Crater Lake National Park is established as the state's first and only national park.

EVENT

state on the Oregon Trail. About 10 percent of the people in Oregon are Hispanic. Asian Americans, African Americans, and American Indians also make up a small percentage of the state's population.

Oregonians spend a lot of time reading. In fact, people in Portland read more than people in almost any other U.S. city. Among the books Oregonians can choose from are ones by authors from their home state. Ken Kesey is a famous Oregon author. His novels *One Flew Over the Cuckoo's Nest* and *Sometimes a Great Notion* were made into movies. Another Oregon author, Beverly Cleary, is well known for such children's books as those about a character named Ramona Quimby.

Another notable Oregonian was Linus Carl Pauling, one of the most important scientists of the 20th century. Pauling received the Nobel Prize in Chemistry for 1954. He was also awarded the 1962 Nobel Peace Prize for his efforts to end the testing of nuclear weapons.

Descendants of Oregon Trail pioneers, such as this woman, treasure the family stories that have been passed on.

Linus Pauling spent his adult life studying what matter—from rocks to blood—is made of.

YEAR

1937   The Bonneville Dam is completed, becoming the first dam on the Columbia River.

EVENT

Oregon Outdoors

Oregon's natural beauty draws outdoor enthusiasts to the state. Every year, millions of visitors travel to Oregon's rocky coast. In 1967, the state passed a law that made almost the entire coastline open to the public. This means that people can walk along the shore wherever they want to.

Although the water is usually too cold for swimming, visitors to the coast can enjoy looking out to sea. In December, people gather along Oregon's coast to watch gray whales swimming south. In the spring, the whales can be seen journeying north with their young. Volunteers staff some of the best whale-watching sites, including Ecola, Seal Rock, and Harris Beach state parks. They help visitors spot the huge animals.

The Oregon Dunes National Recreation Area provides a 40-mile-long (64 km) natural "sandbox" along the coast of central Oregon. The dunes in this area rise up to 500 feet (152 m) above sea level. Many visitors hike up and down the dunes. Others prefer the adventure of driving motorcycles and 4 x 4s over the sandy hills.

Farther inland, Oregon's forests, mountains, and rivers offer opportunities for camping, skiing, mountain biking, fishing, and hunting. Mount Hood in the Cascade Mountains is the only place in North America that offers year-round skiing. Dressed in T-shirts, skiers can swoosh down the Palmer

Haystack Rock (opposite), a well-known sea stack at Cannon Beach, and the sand dunes (above) are some of the state's natural attractions.

YEAR

1971   Oregon becomes one of the first states to ban the sale of non-returnable beverage bottles.

EVENT

- 25 -

The Portland Trail Blazers began play in 1970 and have since become a beloved part of the city.

snowfield in 70 °F (21 °C) weather. Many Olympic athletes use Mount Hood as a summer training ground.

In addition to being a skier's paradise, Mount Hood is one of the most climbed mountains in North America. Every year, 5,000 people attempt to reach the summit, or top, of this mountain. Many reach the summit safely, but climbing the mountain is risky. In the past 100 years, about 130 people have died attempting the climb.

Those interested in incredible depths rather than amazing heights can visit the Columbia River Gorge on Oregon's border with Washington. One 12-mile (19 km) stretch of the gorge contains 11 waterfalls, including the spectacular Mult-nomah Falls. With a drop of 620 feet (190 m), this waterfall is the second-tallest year-round waterfall in the U.S.

In addition to outdoor activities, the people of Oregon like to spend time watching professional sports. Loyal fans of the National Basketball Association's Portland Trail Blazers pack the Rose Garden Arena for home games. Oregon also hosts minor-league soccer, baseball, and hockey teams. In addition, many runners live and train in the city of Eugene, which is called "The Track Capital of the World."

Multnomah Falls, located in Larch Mountain, is part of the Columbia River Gorge National Scenic Area.

YEAR

1996   Major flooding causes millions of dollars of damage to homes and businesses in the Willamette Valley.

EVENT

T he name of Oregon's only professional sports team, the Trail Blazers, honors the pioneers who first traveled the Oregon Trail. Today, visitors to the End of the Oregon Trail Interpretive Center in Oregon City can experience what life was like for those early settlers. Hands-on activities allow tourists to try their hand at packing a wagon and making candles. They can imagine what it was like to be some of the first people to see the wild land.

Oregon retains much of the wildness that the first settlers discovered. Yet many Oregonians are concerned that continued logging, fishing, industrial development, and recreational activities are endangering the land. They are working hard to find ways to preserve Oregon's natural beauty for generations to come.

Two images that are closely associated with Oregon are the covered wagons on display at the End of the Oregon Trail Interpretive Center (above) and the stunning Mount Hood (opposite).

1941   Oregon becomes the first state to require that trees be replanted after logging or natural disasters.

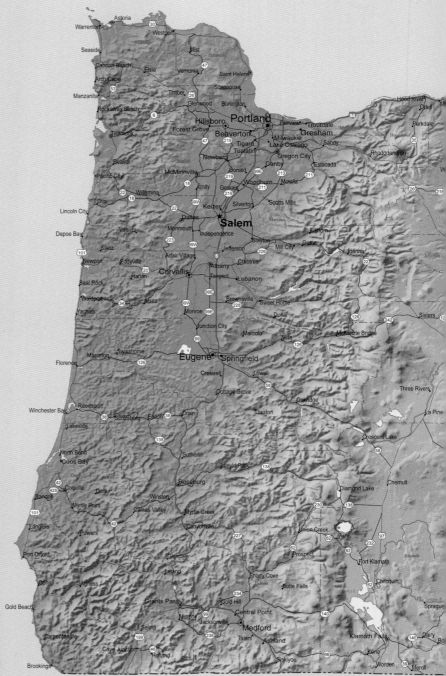

QUICK FACTS

Population: 3,747,455

Largest city: Portland (pop. 550,396)

Capital: Salem

Entered the union: February 14, 1859

Nickname: Beaver State

State flower: Oregon grape

State bird: western meadowlark

Size: 98,381 square miles (254,806 sq km)—9th-biggest in U.S.

Major industries: logging, agriculture, tourism, manufacturing, technology

YEAR

2002   A forest fire caused by lightning burns thousands of acres of Oregon forestland.

EVENT

BIBLIOGRAPHY

Dary, David. *The Oregon Trail: An American Saga*. New York: Alfred A. Knopf, 2004.

Dunegan, Lizann. *Insiders' Guide to the Oregon Coast*. Guilford, Conn.: Insiders' Guide, 2007.

Highberger, Mark. *An Explorer's Guide: Oregon*. Woodstock, Vt.: The Countryman Press, 2006.

Samson, Karl. *Frommer's Oregon*. Hoboken, N.J.: Wiley Publishing, 2006.

Warren, Stuart, and Ted Long Ishikawa. *Oregon Handbook*. Chico, Calif.: Moon Publications, 1998.

INDEX